A Nihilist's Bible

Stewart Storrar

Stewart Storrar

Nihilist's Bible

Published by Lore Publication in 2022.

Copyright © Stewart Storrar, 2022.

All rights reserved. No part of this book may be reproduced in any form or by an electronic or mechanical means, including information storage and retrieval systems, without permission in writing from the publisher, except by a reviewer who may quote brief passages in a review.

To request permissions, contact the publisher at:
lorepublications@gmail.com

ISBN: 978-1-7397218-0-0

@lorepublication

lorepublication.com

Stewart Storrar

Nihilist's Bible

To:

A better day.

Stewart Storrar

Contents

FORWARD   11

I   13

II   14

III   16

IV   18

V   22

VI   23

VII   23

VIII   25

IX   26

X   27

XI   29

XII   31

XIII	**32**
XIV	**33**
XV	**35**
XVI	**36**
XVII	**37**
XVIII	**38**
XIX	**40**
XX	**41**
XXI	**43**
XXII	**45**
XXIII	**46**
XXIV	**48**
XXV	**49**
XXVI	**50**
XXVII	**51**

XXVIII	51
XXIX	53
XXX	54
XXXI	55
XXXII	56
XXXIII	57
XXXIV	58
XXXV	59
XXXVI	59
XXXVII	62
XXXVIII	63
GOODBYE	64

Stewart Storrar

Forward

In my darkness, I find truth.
In my pain, I find strength.
In my weakness, I find love.
In my fear, I find hope.
In my death, I find freedom.

The only truth is in that of the void,
And in this truth, I find peace.

*

Pain made me,
Pain made you,
The rest is all noise.

*

To you, dear reader, I impart these words.
Not that it matters in the end,
Find peace in them for what it is worth,
And make the most of the now,
Because you'll be a long time dead when it comes.

Stewart Storrar

– Yours, Stewart.

.

Nihilist's Bible

I

I see a thousand eyes,

    I hear a thousand words,

        I feel a thousand ways,

    But what I am,
    Is what I'm not.

And who I am will never matter.

II

Oh, what a wonderful act of wizardry,
A fundamental act of thievery,
To care about a world of banality,
And indulge in the arbitrary.

And then comes the question of purpose,
A question so frivolous and wry,
The grandest deception of all,
Right before your very eyes.

What does it take to see?
The coaxality of life and lie?
The duality of all and nothing,
Living in constant vie.

Yet most refuse to see it,
The crushing paradox of man,
That each life is given freely,
Without a choice in why it began.

Or maybe most don't care to see it.
So, how can one be free?
When two people make a choice,
And bring me into the world to be,
Not for the sake of I,
Only for the sake of thee,
To force their will and wants,
Upon a weary me.

Yes, most don't care to consider,
To be or not to be,
Isn't a question of choice,
When I don't want to be me.

III

When the wonder of ideas,
Of who you should be,
Haunt the mind,
And the demand,
Of the world's cohesive structures,
Drive the human condition,
Is this not a death of the worst kind?

Death should be a freedom,
Not a want,
Or a need.

And when the wonders of ideas,
Of who you should be,
Paralyse the mind with inaction,

Should one not let go of our
insatiable need,
To define the ideas of who we
should be?

Should we not,
In the raging against the darkness,
Focus on who we can be?
Who we are?
Who we want to be?

Is this not freedom?

Freedom to break free.

Freedom,
To just be.

IV

With the clash of a sabre against steel,

And the might of one will against another,

On countless forgotten battlefields,

The winds of change dictate,

That final breath, on that final day,

The reaper of men basks in glory,

As you play the devil's hand in a cosmic story,

Of bound fate and decided destiny.

Or,

With the flash of a gun muzzle,

And the fight of one life against another,

On nameless roads of townships,

The winds of change dictate,

The final decision, in that fleeting moment,

The reaper of men creeps with shame,

As you abuse the devil's hand in a cosmic story,

Of false fate and broken destiny.

Or,

With the lash of your own mind,

And the battle of thought against reason,

On endless epochs of life,

The winds of change dictate,

That final thought, in a transient state,

The reaper of men stalks in grief,

As you fake the devil's hand in a cosmic story,

Of chosen fate and forged destiny.

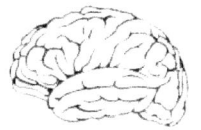

I ask, on that fateful day,

When the dust settles,

And the wind halts,

And the reaper waits,

Who have you become?

And who will you continue to be?

V

Once a raging tempest of opinion,
Now tame.

Once a fire worthy of brimstone,
Now extinguished.

Once a lightning spark of hope,
Now diffused.

This world,
It once was,
Now, it's not.

Yet all you see is you.

VI

It is the tree rustling in the shrill wind,
The amber leaf that falls from the tree,
The loose rock from the rigid cliff face,
The rogue cloud in a clear sky.

It is the smouldering ash,
To the raging flames.

The mighty sword,
To the broken shield.

What I am is your perfect chaos.

The chaos you refuse to face.

VII

Can you feel it?
That wisp of a soul searching,
Forever wandering the wastelands of love.

The ignorance of the loveless,
And forsaken bravery of the loved.

The venom of the unloved,
Corrupts the idea of purity.

They can feel it,
Have felt it.

Have you?

VIII

Time is a unique enigma,

A resource of life one can never get back,

Yet a resource of life one can fail to spend.

Human nature is to want more of what we cannot have,

Yet time is never wanted,

Only wasted.

IX

Tis' but a twist of fate,
I hear you say.

      The world on fire,
      Our souls astray.

          To what end I ask you now,
            Do we change our ways?

And so the fire flays,
The armour of kings,
And the water betrays,
The closest of kin.

All you do in your castles of clay,
Is dwindle, hide, hope, and pray.

X

Only in the eyes of a true believer,
Can one ever be saved.

Only in the mind of the saved,
Can the seed be sown.

A seed of doubt and fear,
A seed to govern,
A seed to rape.

Only in the eyes of a true believer,
Can your voice be heard,
Or are your words destined to fall on deaf ears?

What be you?
But one lonely sheep in a herd,
And then comes the dawn,
With the time for shearing drawing nigh.

*Only in the eyes of a true believer,
Is your blindness, a sight.*

*So ask your questions,
Imbibe those lies,
Bend that knee,
And give away your life.*

XI

To the ballad of the lonesome bard,
Whose song echoes through desolate streets.

To the musings of a forgotten writer,
Whose scribes are lost to time.

To the brush stroke of a fameless artist,
Whose canvas knows no eyes.

The void calls,
In an enigma of twisted fate,
And tomb of shattered dreams,
Waiting to estrange the mind,
To that which can never be known,
But always pondered.

In this perfect uncertainty,
Of a strange world,
The bard sings,
The writer writes,
And the artist paints,
For whatever will and forever be,
Our forlorn memories.

XII

What world is it?
This one of pain and sorrow?
Is it a world of life lived?
Or perhaps,
It is a world of choice.

What world is it?
This one of bliss and joy?
Is it a world of life lived?
Or perhaps,
Is it a world of choice?

What world is it?
This world of choice?
If nothing but a world chosen.

Nihilist's Bible

XIII

It's that feeling,
That darkness you refuse to face,
That anger that rots your mind,
That fear that corrupts your hope,
That pain that gives you strength.

What is that feeling,
But a seed of known truth,
Sown in a field of humanity,
For only the cursed to tend.

And yet it flowers.

XIV

I ask,
What kind of world do we live in?
If not one of temptation?

I ask,
To what end do we quell our truest wants?
For that of a safe future?

I ask,
What life is one to lead?
In the shroud of what could be?
Stalked by that which you can never know.

I ask,
Why does this life have to be?
When all that one desires,
Is that which can never be had.

I ask,
Why shouldn't the void take me?
When suffering seems to be,
All that I have known.

Nihilist's Bible

But now,
I no longer ask.

Now,
I just am.

XV

Here I stand,
On the edge of apocalypse,
To what turn of fate,
Do I owe thanks?

I can feel it,
The dust of yesteryear,
And ash of anamnesis,
Burying me,
With a life I never knew,
Friends I've never had,
And places I've never been.

For what are we, if not born to suffer?
To stand idle on the shore of life,
As the tide of the void draws ever closer.

All I seem to ponder,
Is to what agent do I owe,
And to what extent I shall know,
The truest madness of a sane mind?

XVI

Can you feel it?
That omnipotent feeling,
Of sinking through the quicksands of time,
With not a care in the world.

Only to realize one fateful day,
That the hands are ticking,
Bringing each second to bare,
And each moment to fruition,
In the hourglass of life,
For which you are but a mere grain,
In the sands of the cosmos.

Only then,
Buried by the sands of time,
Does each second become a relic,
And each moment become a tomb,
To all that you have been,
And all that which you will never be.

XVII

Let the flames of your scorn burn hot,
And the cinders of your hate sizzle,
But let the seed of your love flower fully,
And the roots of your hope grow deep,
To embrace that which you know,
Is as pure,
As the truest form of your self.

For in the mind's eye,
Is *thee* cosmic symmetry,
Of all that will ever be,
And all that can ever be,
Remembered forever,
And forgotten eternally,
Resigned to the fate of a timeless place.

As it was from the dirt of life we were forged,
And to the ashes of death we shall return.

XVIII

What a fruitless endeavour it seems to be,
To concern oneself with being free,
When the mindless madness of the world today,
Offers ample choice for the reaper's prey.

Aye,

Darkness stalks even the purest man,
No matter his pride, posture, or clan.
So in this truth we'll find our peace,
Given to us from fate's lease.

But,

We rage against the the dying light,
In that love, hate, and forlorned flight,
That beyond the darkness is a beacon of hope,
Brought to us by the end of a rope.

Stewart Storrar

Yet,

The stubborn nature that wills us to be,
Is all that persists in the heart of thee,
To swindle, hope, hurt, and pray,
That for a glimpse of a moment we'll find our way.

And so one can never truly know,
All that will come in spite and woe,
Until the day arrives of our parting breath,
To finally embrace the calm of death.

XIX

I see the course of life's river,
Winding away to an ocean,
Of countless possibilities,
In a finite meaningless existence,
And I see the world for what it is,
A monstrous vista of absurdity,
And before the long dark,
On the crest of morality,
My awareness of this unshakable truth,
That the world and therein holds no meaning,
Stands as my very reason,
And my conscious choice,
To choose to experience,
This enigma of life,
As a meaningful one.

Life has no meaning,
And in this revelation,
I find mine.

XX

You're akin to a teardrop in a downpour,
Like a blade of grass in a meadow,
Like a stone on a beach,
A brick in a city,
A coin in a mint,
An atom in the cosmos.

You are but a human,
Among human kind.

You are but a word in the sempiternal script of the universe,
A note in the melody of purpose.

But one word is to a script,
And one note to a melody,
What one second is to time;
A passing moment,
An accumulation of all before you,
And all that proceeds you.

Nihilist's Bible

In the grand sky of creation,
You are but a forgotten wisp on the wind,
In that you don't matter,
And never will,
Aside from in the now,
In the absurd banality of life,
You are,
And in this now,
You will always be.

And from the banality of life,
Wells a teardrop,
Grows some grass,
Forms a stone,
And a brick,
A coin,
And an atom.

From the banality of life,
Arises you.

A human, of human kind.

XXI

Aye' the beckon calls,
From the deaf ear,
To the blind eye,
To what end?

                        Each flame a fire,
              Every downpour a drizzle,
                Each thought an icon,
                Of only yours to tend.

Aye' the beckon calls,
The song of generations,
The melody of life,
Living in you now.

                        Each gust a breeze,
              Every rumble a tremor,
                Each path you choose,
                    A solemn vow.

Aye' the beckon calls,
The tune of those before,
Each note a symbol,
Of promises shattered.

　　　　　　　　Each tempest a spark,
　　　　　　Every mountain a mound,
　　　　　　Every word you breathe,
　　　　　　Said as if it mattered.

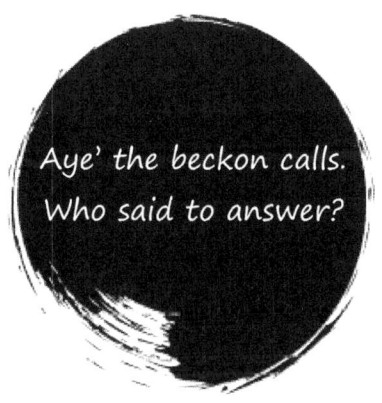

Aye' the beckon calls.
Who said to answer?

Stewart Storrar

XXII

And so,
Let the past die,
I cry,
But you question why?

Is it that,
Upon the eve of meeting the abyss?
That I feel compelled to follow my bliss?
Or condemn my soul to a fateful remiss?

Or is it,
That the heavens cry?
And the reaper is shy?
And my passing nigh?

No,
Your God is a dead, fabled icon,
Your Devil is a fake, scared pawn,
In a world entombed by dusk and dawn.

Yes, I cry,
Let the past die.
Oh, won't you let the past die.

XXIII

A mirror's mask,
Is to us all,
But a fateful quell,
Of the shadow's crawl.

Is life but a dire lie?

Or does the ego feast,
Upon the sheen of hope?
And each reflection,
Grease a lewd slope?

I ask of thee;

Does one not deserve true resolve?
To look past that baneful mirror?
Or does fate will those to be forever questioned,
By life's toughest juror?

But with each gaze the shadow cries.

And upon the eve of each morrow,
You feel the words of the scolder,
Drip down through your very being,
To corrupt the eye of the beholder.

To what end is life a lie?
To what end do I ask of thee?
To what end does the shadow cry?
If not an end forbidden?

XXIV

I surrender, I see,
I sing and slay,
I relish the night,
And scorn the day.

For the woe of man is present in thy,
In darkness, in light, in life, I cry.

For the woe of man is a fearsome creature,
A dark, hidden, serpentine feature.

But it is who I am and who i'll be,
And from this truth, I'll think free.

Because the woe of man is but the will of the way,
And no man, beast, or god may say,

That what lies within is a dark corruption,
When life itself is the seed of destruction.

Yes I surrender, I see,
I sing and slay,
I am a godless instrument,
Of the universe at play.

Stewart Storrar

XXV

Oh, late night ghouls,
Stalkers of dreams,
Bishops of the darkness,
Where do you go when we go?

Do you cackle into the abyss?
Do you howl into the shadows?
Do you hold the hands of the unloved?
And usher a seed of doubt into the mind?

Oh, where do you go?
Yes, where do you go?

XXVI

In a world of scorn and hate,
Of loveless villainy,
Of tyrant godheads,
All that matters is conviction.

Conviction to realize your truth.

XXVII

It is like,
The silk touch of the wind before a storm,
Stealing away a lone teardrop,
Only to replace it with a downpour.

Yet you smile. And I dance anyway.

XXVIII

To feel the ashes of what once was,
Rise up and char your skin,
And feel the acrid scent of defeat,
Choke your weary soul,
It is but a blessing,
And a curse,
To stand tall above the graves of so many,
And shrink before the graves of many more.

Oh, to feel the scourge of battle,
Soak your heart in blood,
And feel the bonds of unity,
Bind your being to the dirt,
It is but a gift,
And a burden,
To claw your path from death's door,
From which many never return.
And you still stand before it,
Blinded by its terrible awe,
Deafened by its harrowing screams,
Guided to never again suffer,
Through the gates of hell on Earth.

War never changes,
Nor the minds of men driving it.

XXIX

In what eye does the world seem fragile,
A trained eye of scorn?
A naïve eye of hope?

Or no eye at all?

Maybe, just maybe,
The world is fragile regardless,
And our eyes stare on nonetheless.

XXX

From the depths of the deepest ocean,
And to the heights of the highest moor,
From the deathly cold of winter,
To the pleasant warmth of summer,
The course of life is sempiternal,
And no God nor man may own it.

For life is about being,
And each moment is to be.

Stewart Storrar

XXXI

How do you hope to live,
In the strangeness of all that is?
In a kamikaze world of absurdity?
Charading as a world of harmony.

And why do you hope to live,
For what purpose do you choose to breathe?
In a disillusioned societal structure,
Almost willing itself to fracture.

Maybe asking how has no need,
And asking why guilts the troubled soul,
Into wanting a state that you never find,
And needing a state to feel at all designed.

Yes,

How do you hope to live?
Why do you hope to live?
When living is what's killing you.

XXXII

I am.
And I must be,
But being is an act,
Of the greatest deception,
Thrust upon thee.

Yes I am,
And that can only be,
The truest calling,
Void of purpose,
For all to see.

So what am I?
What can I be?
Will I wane?
Or will I flee?

Can I live?
Can I be free?
Can I feign?
Or can I see?

XXXIII

And how?
How until a solemn vow,
How until you break a bow,
How until you endow,
How until you wow!

And now?
Now you hang your brow,
Now you condemn but allow,
Now, somehow,
You are all but thou.

But.
How?

XXXIV

Each step,
A thousand paces,

      Each word,
    A thousand phrases,

            Each life,
          A thousand places.

All through vanity,
Escaping from banality,
Avoiding the finality,
Of our inane being.

And that, to me, is the beauty of life.

XXXV

For which soulful sin will you feel hell's brimstone,
And for which act of charity will you feel God's wrath?

What do you say to the limbless child?
Or to the loveless lust of the incel?

How do you feed yourself before the starving?
How can you curse the rains of fate?

To what end does this life have meaning?
If not to fuel a pyrrhic battle,
That will know no moment of victory.

XXXVI

Don't allow,
The waters of praise,
Nor the flames of criticism,
To tarnish your ego.

Don't allow,
A world of luxury,
Nor a world of poverty,
To turn you sour.

The only thing,
You can know as truth,
Is who you are,
And who you chose to be.

And in an absurd world,
True wealth lies,
In the freedom,
That your certain doom can bring.

Stewart Storrar

So don't swindle it,
Celebrate it,
And enjoy every step,
In your soul bound path,
Towards the unavoidable.

Embrace the death of life,
For in death life finds meaning.

XXXVII

I see,
The ocean of the city,
The currents of the people,
The waters of life.

So I reach out.

But my thoughts are a drop in this ocean,
And my voice lost in this riptide of a current.

It seems to me,
That in these waters of life,
I am drowning,
Without a hope of land in sight.

Yet I swim anyway.

Stewart Storrar

XXXVIII

Nothing's forever,
Yet in the fields of what once was,
I see the amaranthine bloom of love,
Corrupted by thorns of lust,
Lost to fantasies of want.

But,
I see it now.

That nothing's forever,
And it never was.

Goodbye

Thank you for reading. Be sure to leave a review on your chosen platform, and use these words for good.

Feel free to connect with me on social media, and follow Lore Publication for my future releases.

Until next time, keep living and keep loving.

About The Author

Stewart, at the time of this work, lives and works from his home city of Glasgow, Scotland. He was born in Rutherglen, 1997, but grew up in the countryside outside the city of Glasgow itself. His childhood and teenage years were spent wandering the outdoors, enjoying nature, and indulging in his various hobbies.

His hobbies include skateboarding, playing the odd video game, star gazing, bushcraft, thinking too much, and delving into the various fictional worlds that TV shows, books, and films have to offer him.

Nihilist's Bible stands as the first full-length completed work from the young writer and has been in development since his late teenage years. It presents itself as a collection of his thoughts about life, love, heartbreak, and his confused curiosity about the world around him. He has struggled with his true identity and mental illness all his life, which has had a heavy influence on his perspective on the world.

Lastly, to end on a cheerful note, he loves ducks, cats, dogs, and has always wanted to visit Nepal!

Stewart Storrar

Printed in Great Britain
by Amazon